HOUSTON PUBLIC LIBRARY

W9-AOP-777

REVIEW COPY
COURTESY OF
ENSLOW PUBLISHERS, INC

Celebrating
THE OBAMA
FAMILY
in Pictures

Jane Katirgis

Enslow Publishers, Inc.
40 Industrial Road
Box 398
Berkeley Heights, NJ 07922
USA
http://www.enslow.com

For my "first" family—
Mom, Dad, Catherine, and Richie

Copyright © 2010 by Enslow Publishers, Inc.

All rights reserved.

No part of this book may be reproduced by any means without the written permission of the publisher.

Library of Congress Cataloging-in-Publication Data

Katirgis, Jane.
 Celebrating the Obama family in pictures / Jane Katirgis.
    p. cm. — (The Obama family photo album)
 Includes bibliographical references and index.
 ISBN-13: 978-0-7660-3653-6
 ISBN-10: 0-7660-3653-7
 1. Obama, Barack—Family—Pictorial works—Juvenile literature. 2. Presidents—United States—Family—Pictorial works—Juvenile literature. I. Title.
 E909.K38 2010
 973.932092—dc22

                            2009013108

Printed in the United States of America

10 9 8 7 6 5 4 3 2 1

To Our Readers:
We have done our best to make sure all Internet Addresses in this book were active and appropriate when we went to press. However, the author and the publisher have no control over and assume no liability for the material available on those Internet sites or on other Web sites they may link to. Any comments or suggestions can be sent by e-mail to comments@enslow.com or to the address on the back cover.

♻ Enslow Publishers, Inc., is committed to printing our books on recycled paper. The paper in every book contains 10% to 30% post-consumer waste (PCW). The cover board on the outside of each book contains 100% PCW. Our goal is to do our part to help young people and the environment too!

Photo Credits: Associated Press, pp. 4, 6, 7, 8 (bottom), 11 (top), 12, 14, 16, 18, 19, 20, 21, 22, 23, 24–25, 26, 27, 30; Eric Thayer/Reuters/Landov, p. 17; Jason Reed/Reuters/Landov, pp. 3, 28; Jim Young/Reuters/Landov, p. 9; Keith Bedford/Reuters/Landov, p. 10; Kevin Dietsch/UPI /Landov, p. 31; Michael Reynolds/UPI /Landov, p. 1; Oliver Douliery/MCT/Landov, p. 11 (bottom); Pete Souza/The White House/Polaris, p. 8 (top); White House Photo by Pete Souza, pp. 5, 15, 29.

Cover Photo: Associated Press (front); White House Photo by Pete Souza (back).

Contents

Barack, Sasha, Malia, and Michelle Obama appear on stage at the Democratic National Convention in Denver, Colorado, on August 28, 2008.

First Family

On August 28, 2008, Barack Obama accepted the nomination to run for president. More than a year later, after campaigning across the country, he won the election.

On January 20, 2009, the first family moved into the White House to start their new life in Washington, D.C. Daughters Malia, age 10, and Sasha, age 7, settled into their new home and a new school. It had been quite a journey, starting when Barack Obama began his career in politics in Chicago, Illinois.

President Obama and his daughters at the White House.

5

Starting Out in Chicago

*B*arack Obama and Michelle Robinson were married on October 18, 1992 in Chicago, Illinois. Barack began a career in politics, first as an Illinois State Senator, and then as a United States Senator.

Their daughters, Sasha (left) and Malia, join Barack and Michelle as they wait for the votes to be counted for the 2004 election for U.S. Senator. Obama won the election.

Malia

Malia Ann Obama was born on July 4, 1998. She enjoys taking photographs. Here she takes a picture of her father as he gets ready to go to his inaugural ball. Her sister, Sasha, jumps for joy.

On her ninth birthday, Malia pretends to sing into a microphone as her father greets supporters during a party in Iowa. ▶

Sasha

Natasha Obama, known as Sasha, was born on June 7, 2001. She is the youngest person to live in the White House since John F. Kennedy, Jr., in 1961.

Sasha has fun at a rehearsal before the Democratic National Convention in Denver, Colorado, August 25, 2008. She is standing at the podium where her mom will give a speech later that evening.

Visit to Africa

Barack Obama's father was born in Africa. The Obama family took a trip there in August 2006. They planted an African olive tree at Uhuru Park in Nairobi, Kenya. Sasha and her dad use the shovel, while Malia and Nobel Peace Prize-winner Wangari Maathai hold the tree.

Family Fun

*S*asha and her dad ride bumper cars at the Iowa State Fair in August 2007.

*M*alia and Sasha enjoy sleigh riding with their mom at the White House in March 2009.

Community Service

$\mathcal{M}$ichelle Obama and her daughters pack care packages for troops in Iraq. ▶

$\mathcal{P}$resident-elect Barack Obama hugs a visitor as he and his family give out Thanksgiving turkeys at a food bank in Chicago in 2008.

Campaign Trail

When Senator Barack Obama decided to run for president, he and his family visited many states in the country. Here, they gather on stage before Barack makes a speech at a campaign stop in Iowa. ▶

The Obama family talks with a young boy as Barack campaigns door-to-door in Indiana.

Family Fitness

*T*he Obamas enjoy exercising as a family. Barack and Michelle help their daughters, Malia (left) and Sasha, roller-skate at Great Skates Fun Center in Lafayette, Indiana.

*S*asha and her dad enjoy a Sunday bike ride in Chicago. The city was their home before they moved to Washington, D.C.

Hawaiian Vacation

*B*arack Obama spends time on the beach with Malia and Sasha during a vacation to Hawaii. Barack lived in Hawaii with his grandparents from the time he was ten years old until he went to college.

*D*ad, Sasha, and Malia enjoy a shaved ice treat during vacation in Kailua, Hawaii.

Reunion on the Campaign Trail

$\mathcal{D}$uring his campaign for president, Barack Obama traveled from state to state, often without his family. They were always happy to see him again. Just days before the election, they greet him as he gets off a plane in Colorado.

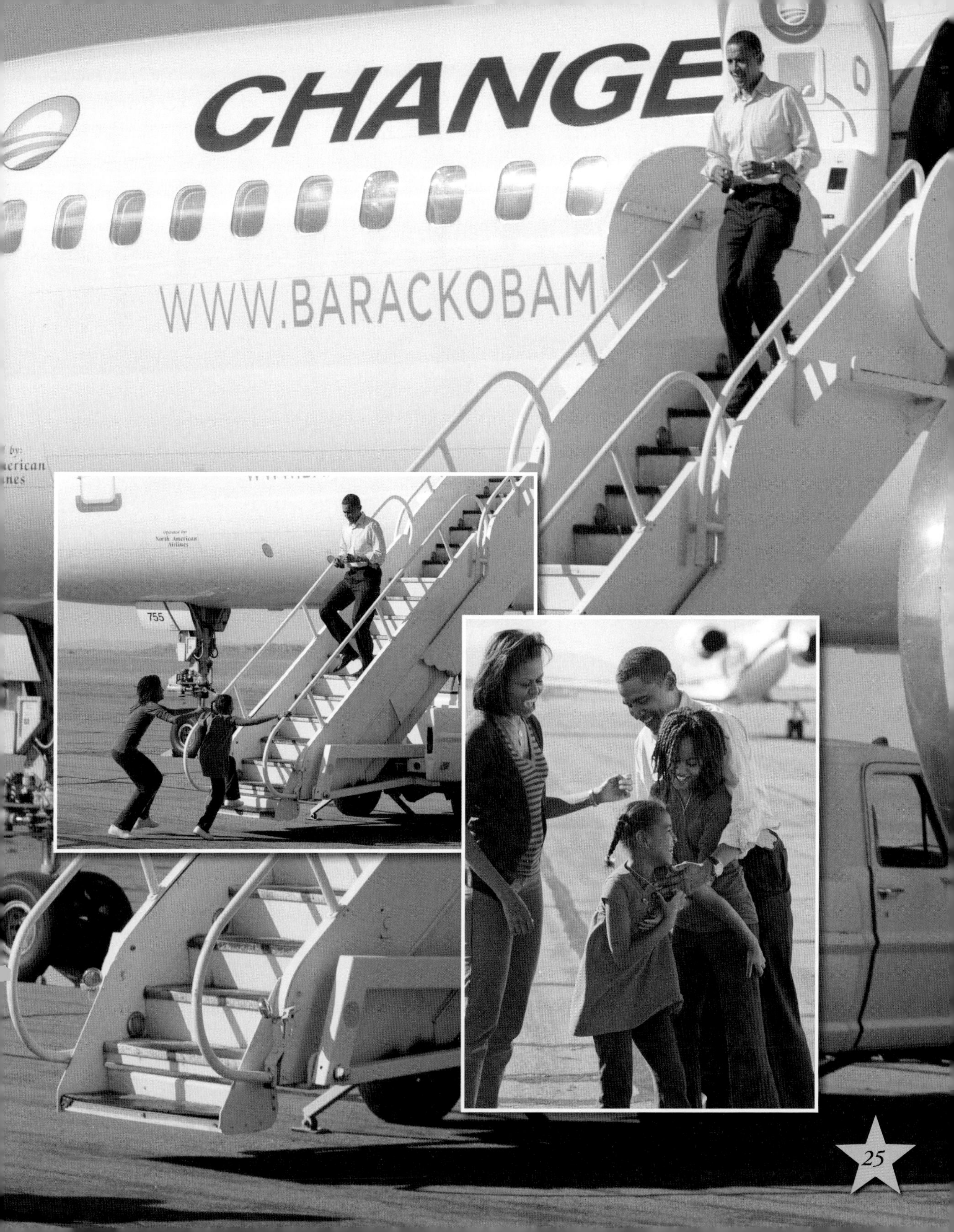
CHANGE
WWW.BARACKOBAM
North American
Airlines
755

It was an exciting day for the family when Barack Obama was sworn in as the 44th president of the United States. Barack, Michelle, Malia, and Sasha stood before a crowd of more than one million people at the U.S. Capitol on January 20, 2009.

Inauguration Day

*M*alia (in blue) and Sasha join their grandmother, Marian Robinson (left), and aunt, Maya Soetoro-Ng, at the inauguration. Robinson is Michelle's mother. She moved into the White House to help take care of the girls. Soetoro-Ng is Barack Obama's sister.

At Home in the White House

Sasha leads her family off the Marine One helicopter. They are returning from a weekend trip. The helicopter lets them off onto the South Lawn of the White House.

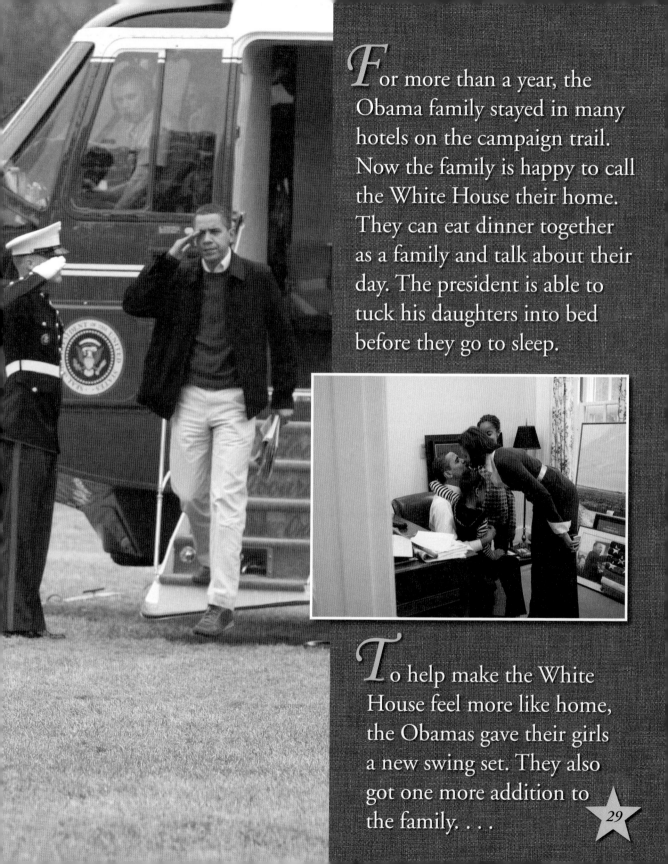

For more than a year, the Obama family stayed in many hotels on the campaign trail. Now the family is happy to call the White House their home. They can eat dinner together as a family and talk about their day. The president is able to tuck his daughters into bed before they go to sleep.

To help make the White House feel more like home, the Obamas gave their girls a new swing set. They also got one more addition to the family. . . .

Malia Obama runs with Bo on the South Lawn of the White House.

A New Addition to the Family

*A*fter Barack Obama won the 2008 presidential election, he promised Malia and Sasha a new puppy. In April 2009, the family welcomed Bo, a six-month-old Portuguese water dog, to the White House.

*T*he whole family enjoys having a pet. It's just one more thing that makes the White House feel like home.

Further Reading

Books

Brophy, David Bergen. *Michelle Obama: Meet the First Lady*. New York: HarperCollins, 2008.

Grimes, Nikki. *Barack Obama: Son of Promise, Child of Hope*. New York: Simon & Schuster Books for Young Readers, 2008.

O'Connor, Jane. *If the Walls Could Talk: Family Life at the White House*. New York: Simon & Schuster Books for Young Readers, 2004.

Internet Addresses

Kids.gov. *The Official Kids' Portal for the U.S. Government.*
http://www.kids.gov

White House 101. *Facts and Fun for All Ages.*
http://www.whitehouse.gov/about/white_house_101/

Index

+
973.932 K

Katirgis, Jane.
Celebrating the Obama family
in pictures
Central Kids CIRC - 4th fl
12/09

Friends of the
Houston Public Library